To: Soledad

For: Being a Wonderful Friend

Date: July 11, 2009

¡AMIGAS FOREVER!

Artwork by

Luis Fitch

H®

HARVEST HOUSE PUBLISHERS

EUGENE, OREGON

¡Amigas Forever!

Copyright © 2009 by Harvest House Publishers
Eugene, Oregon 97402
www.harvesthousepublishers.com

ISBN 978-0-7369-2486-3

Artwork © by Luis Fitch and used by Harvest House Publishers, Inc., under authorization from MHS Licensing, Minneapolis, Minnesota. For more information regarding art prints featured in this book, please contact:

> MHS Licensing
> 11100 Wayzata Blvd., Suite 550
> Minneapolis, MN 55305
> (952) 544-1377
> www.mhslicensing.com

Design and production by Garborg Design Works, Savage, Minnesota

Printed in China

09 10 11 12 13 14 15 / LP / 10 9 8 7 6 5 4 3 2 1

Contents

Una amiga is someone we turn to when our spirits need a lift,
Una amiga is someone we treasure, for our friendship is a gift.
Una amiga is someone who fills our lives with beauty, joy, and grace
And makes the world we live in a better and happier place.

Author Unknown

Amigas Forever

Dime con quién andas y te diré quién eres.

Tell me with whom you walk and I will tell you who you are.

SPANISH PROVERB

Clothes may make the man, but friends make the woman. A true amiga is irreplaceable. She tells you when it's time to lose the velvet sweat suit and brings you chocolate when life gets too "real." She is essential support and comic relief. You may have grown up in different states or be fluent in different languages, but you now complete each other's sentences. Her influence makes you a better person. You will be amigas forever!

Nothing opens the heart like a true friend, to whom you may impart griefs, joys, fears, hopes…and whatever lies upon the heart.

FRANCIS BACON

True friends are always together in spirit.

LUCY MAUD MONTGOMERY

The best in me and the best in you
Hailed each other because they knew
That always and always since life began
Our being friends was part of God's plan.

GEORGE WEBSTER DOUGLAS

Para amigos, todos;
para enemigos,
uno solo.

One enemy is too
many; and a hundred
friends too few.

SPANISH PROVERB

Besides God Himself, I have no more devoted friend or companion in my life than my journal. I take her everywhere I go, spend time with her, pour out my heart to her, share my burdens and cares, let her see me at my best and worst. I entrust my soul to her keeping. She guards my secrets and lovingly holds my heart. She knows all the dreams I ever dared to entertain.

LUCI SWINDOLL

Amigos son besos soplados por los ángeles.

Friends are kisses blown to us by angels.

The heartfelt counsel of a friend is as sweet as perfume and incense.

THE BOOK OF PROVERBS

Nena, what an amazing gift you are to my life. *¡Qué suerte* am I that you call me friend! *Amiga mía,* you are truly a blessing to me. *Te adoro.*

VERONICA CURTIS

*It is by loving
and by being
loved that
one can come
nearest to the
soul of another.*

GEORGE MACDONALD

No love, no
friendship can
cross the path
of our destiny
without leaving
some mark
on it forever.

FRANÇOIS MAURIAC

Nothing but heaven itself is better
than a friend who is really a friend.

PLAUTUS

Genuine friendship develops
not because we think there will
be a benefit from it but because
of an almost tangible feeling of
connection that recognizes an
affinity between two people.
Friendships are built on mutual
interest. Built on personality. Built
on common experience. That is
why friendships can develop in
the workplace very nicely. We have
a lot of common experiences.

NELLA BARKLEY

*Una vida sin amigos parece
una muerte sin testigos.*

Life without a friend is like
death without a witness.

13

No Translation Needed

Al buen entendedor, pocas palabras bastan.

To the good "understander," few words are needed.

SPANISH PROVERB

The language of friendship is universal. It doesn't require a specific alphabet or special inflections. It merely requires understanding, laughter, companionship, and genuine caring. A hug, a smile, a roll of the eyes doesn't need a translator. Friendship transcends differences in culture and language. When true amigas get together, it's the similarities that count.

It seems to me that trying to live without friends is like milking a bear to get cream for your morning coffee. It is a whole lot of trouble, and then not worth much after you get it.

ZORA NEALE HURSTON

How rare and wonderful is that flash of a moment when we realize we have discovered a friend.

WILLIAM E. ROTHSCHILD

There are three types of
friends: Those like food,
without which you can't live;
those like medicine, which
you need occasionally; and
those like an illness, which
you never want.

SOLOMON IBN GABIROL

The true way and the
sure way to friendship
is through humility—
being open to each
other, accepting each
other just as we are,
knowing each other.

MOTHER TERESA

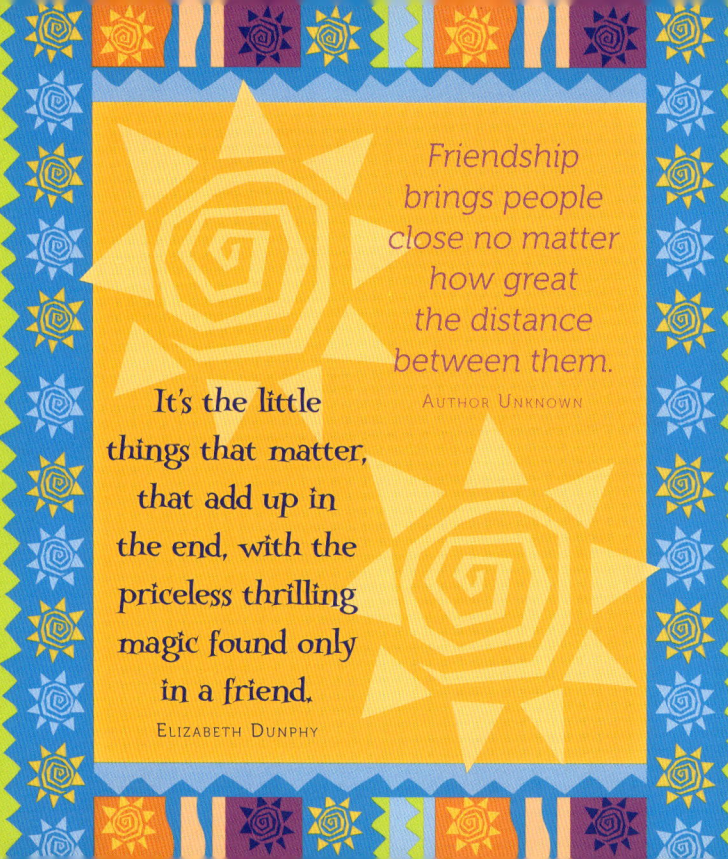

Friendship brings people close no matter how great the distance between them.

AUTHOR UNKNOWN

It's the little things that matter, that add up in the end, with the priceless thrilling magic found only in a friend.

ELIZABETH DUNPHY

Having someone who understands is a great blessing for ourselves. Being someone who understands is a great blessing to others.

JANETTE OKE

The language of friendship is not words but meaning.

HENRY DAVID THOREAU

There is one friend in the life of each of us who seems not a separate person, however dear and beloved, but an expansion, an interpretation, of one's self, the very meaning of one's soul.

EDITH WHARTON

Quién a buen árbol se arrima
buena sombra le cobija.

Whoever leans close to a
good tree is blanketed by
good shade.

SPANISH PROVERB

*To know someone here or there
with whom you feel there is an
understanding in spite of distances
or thoughts unexpressed—that can
make of this earth a garden.*

GOETHE

You have done it without a touch.
Without a word, without a sign.
You have done it by being yourself.
Perhaps that is what being a friend is.

ROY CROFT

I Am Who I Am

Many people will walk in and out of your life, but only true friends will leave footprints in your heart.

ELEANOR ROOSEVELT

Where you come from is reflected in who you are. Whether you are from a passionate Latin culture where hugs are plentiful or a Scandinavian culture where hugs are reserved for special moments, your uniqueness adds depth to your friendships. Let your culture shine through. Your amigas will embrace you for being you.

Perfume and incense
bring joy to the heart,
and the pleasantness of
one's friend springs from
his earnest counsel.

THE BOOK OF PROVERBS

The most beautiful
discovery true
friends make is
that they can grow
separately without
growing apart.

ELISABETH FOLEY

*A friend is someone
who understands
your past, believes
in your future, and
accepts you today
just the way you are.*

BEVERLY LAHAYE

Wherever you
are, it is your
own friends
who make
your world.

WILLIAM JAMES

An *amiga fiel*
is someone
who says nice
things behind
your back.

AUTHOR UNKNOWN

A true friend is one who is concerned about what we are becoming, who sees beyond the present relationship, and who cares deeply about us as a whole person.

GLORIA GAITHER

Everyone wants to be appreciated, so if you appreciate someone, don't keep it a secret.

MARY KAY ASH

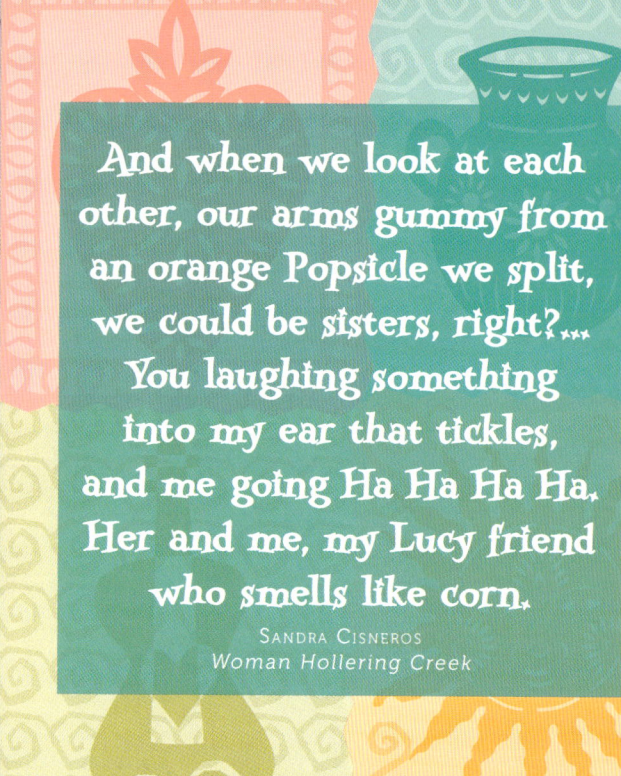

And when we look at each
other, our arms gummy from
an orange Popsicle we split,
we could be sisters, right?...
You laughing something
into my ear that tickles,
and me going Ha Ha Ha Ha.
Her and me, my Lucy friend
who smells like corn.

SANDRA CISNEROS
Woman Hollering Creek

How sweet the sound of friends
laughing together, of sharing the
joy of knowing each other so well.

AUTHOR UNKNOWN

Who we are is connected to those
we love and to those who have
influenced us toward goodness.

CHRISTOPHER DE VINCK

We are all travelers
in the wilderness of
this world, and the
best we can find
in our travels is an
honest friend.

ROBERT LOUIS STEVENSON

*From what we
get, we can
make a living;
what we give,
however,
makes a life.*

ARTHUR ASHE

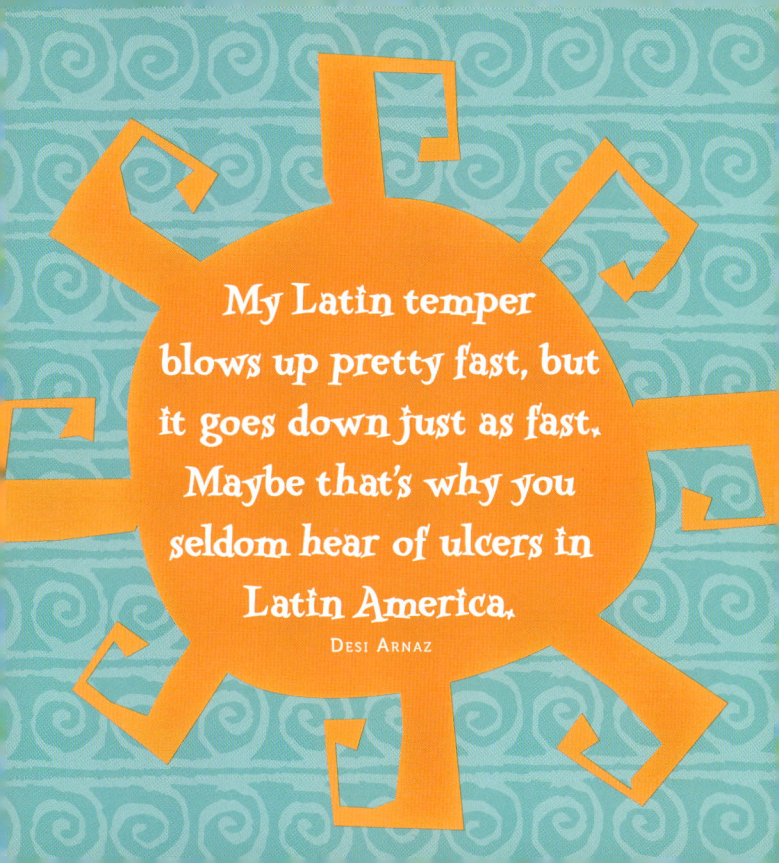

My Latin temper
blows up pretty fast, but
it goes down just as fast.
Maybe that's why you
seldom hear of ulcers in
Latin America.

DESI ARNAZ

A Friend Indeed

Al mal tiempo, buena cara.

Put a nice face to the bad times.

SPANISH PROVERB

When the going gets tough, amigas call their friends. Where else can you get a shoulder to cry on, unwavering support, and free ice cream? True friends are worth their weight in gold. Selected with care, your amigas come to the rescue whether the problem is a broken coffeepot or a broken soul, proving over and over again that a friend in need is a friend indeed.

I want just one thing. To live long enough to pay back in some way your undeserved and overwhelming generosity.

PAM BROWN

I always felt that the great high privilege, relief, and comfort of friendship was that one had to explain nothing.

KATHERINE MANSFIELD

En las malas se conocen a los amigos.

A friend in need is
a friend indeed.

SPANISH PROVERB

One's friends
are that part of
the human race
with which one
can be human.

GEORGE SANTAYANA

It is not so
much our
friends' help
that helps
us as the
confident
knowledge
that they
will help us.

EPICURUS

The friend who holds your
hand and says the wrong thing
is made of dearer stuff than
the one who stays away.

BARBARA KINGSOLVER

A friend can tell you
things you don't want
to tell yourself.

FRANCES WARD WELLER

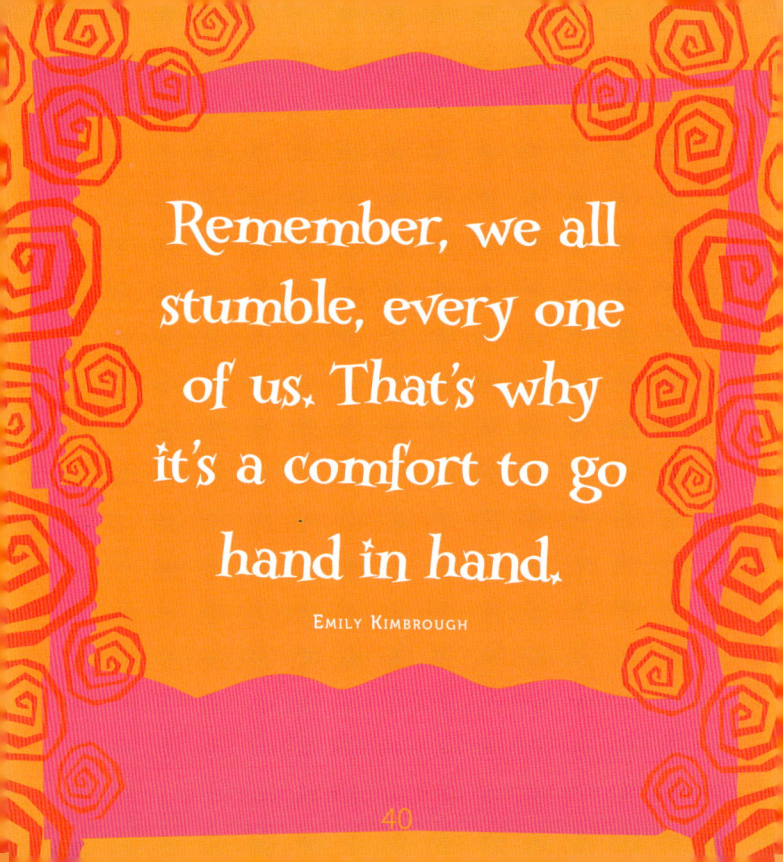

Remember, we all stumble, every one of us. That's why it's a comfort to go hand in hand.

EMILY KIMBROUGH

No matter how my life
changes, my need for
friends continues.

LOIS WYSE

Friendship is a cozy shelter
from life's rainy days.

AUTHOR UNKNOWN

Every true friend is a
glimpse of God.

LUCY LARCOM

What the dew is to the flower,
Gentle words are to the soul.

POLLY RUPE

The most precious of all possessions
is a wise and loyal friend.

DARIUS

Mi Casa Es Su Casa

Más vale llegar a tiempo que ser invitado.

It is better to arrive at the right moment than to be invited.

Welcome. Some people make you feel welcome without even trying. It's not about the house or the decor or the food. It's about how she makes you feel—that her home truly is your home. A safe haven. A place where you know where to find the antibiotic cream, the measuring cups, and the emergency chocolate.

The only way
to have a friend
is to be one.

RALPH WALDO EMERSON

A friend is someone who allows
you distance but is never far away.

NOAH BEN SHEA

Treat your friends as you do
your pictures, and place them
in their best light.

JENNIE JEROME CHURCHILL

You have welcomed
me as your guest;
blessings overflow! Your
goodness and unfailing
kindness shall be with
me all of my life.

THE BOOK OF PSALMS

I love you—
I am at rest with you—
I have come home.

DOROTHY L. SAYERS

When friends are at your
hearthside met,

Sweet courtesy has
done its most

If you have made each
guest forget

That he himself is
not the host.

THOMAS BAILEY ALDRICH

No matter
what your
house looks
like, you let
friends in.

MARY KENT

The human heart,
at whatever age, opens
only to the heart that
opens in return.

MARIA EDGEWORTH

Home. A place where
when you get there,
you know your heart has
been there all along.

GLORIA GAITHER

51

We are lucky when someone places us in the forefront of their busy life and calls to say "hi" or to see what we think about this or that. We are fortunate when someone breathes peace into our lives rather than chaos or competition. We are deeply blessed when someone considers our minds and hearts worthy of further inquiry. And when that person witnesses us on our laziest, slouchiest days and still considers us interesting, well then, that is a forever friend.

PAULINE FLORA

The greatest good you can do for another is not just share your riches, but reveal to them their own.

Benjamin Disraeli

Long years you've kept the door ajar
To greet me, coming from afar.
Long years in my accustomed place
I've read my welcome in your face.

Robert Bridges

A good friend is a connection
to life—a tie to the past, a road
to the future, the key to sanity
in a totally insane world.

Lois Wyse

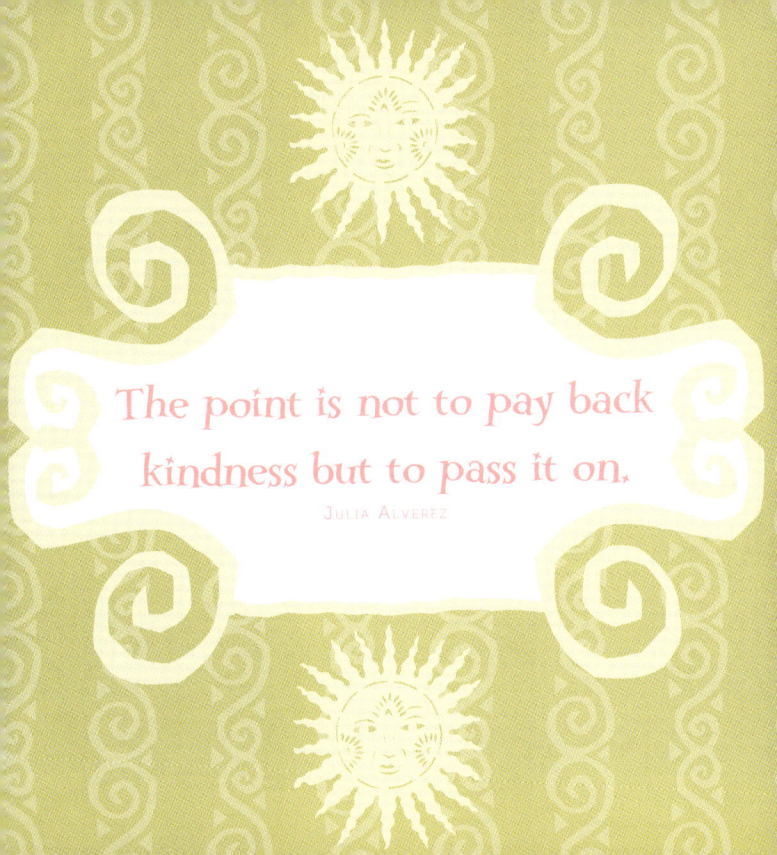

The point is not to pay back
kindness but to pass it on.

JULIA ALVEREZ

Dreams to Share

When we dream alone it remains only a dream.
When we dream together it is not just a dream;
it is the beginning of reality.

DOM HELDER CAMARA

Friends dream together. Some dreams are as simple as wishing for a maid while others are as complex as how to make the world a safer place. Whatever the dream, your amigas help you build it, believe it, and accomplish it. They join in, offer support, and applaud even the smallest successes. And when you dream together, friendship blooms.

*No dejes para mañana
lo que puedas hacer hoy.*

**Don't wait for
tomorrow to do something
you can do today.**

Friendship warms like a
sunbeam; charms like a good
story; inspires like a brave leader;
binds like a golden chain; guides
like a heavenly vision.

NEWELL DWIGHT HILLIS

Plant a seed of friendship;
reap a bouquet of happiness.

Lois L. Kaufman

Real inspiration is something that is always with you. It's about memory. Everything influences you, walking on the street, traveling. I can see a painting and get inspiration from the color.

CAROLINA HERRERA

A friend knows the song in my heart and sings it to me when my memory fails.

DONNA ROBERTS

If instead of a gem, or even a
flower, we should cast the gift
of a loving thought into the heart
of a friend, that would be
giving as the angels give.

GEORGE MACDONALD

Feet, why do I need them
if I have wings to fly?

FRIDA KAHLO

El que busca encuentra.

Look for
something
and you
will find it.

SPANISH PROVERB

*Lift up your eyes.
The heavenly
Father waits to
bless you—in
inconceivable
ways to make
your life what you
never dreamed it
could be.*

ANNE ORTLUND

I awoke
this morning
with devout
thanksgiving
for my
friends, the
old and
the new.

RALPH WALDO EMERSON